Andrew

NEVERMORE

Oxford*Poets*

CARCANET

First published in 2000 by
Carcanet Press Limited
4th Floor, Conavon Court
12-16 Blackfriars Street
Manchester M3 5BQ

A CIP catalogue record for this book
is available from the British Library
ISBN 1 903039 02 9

The publisher acknowledges financial assistance
from the Arts Council of England

Set in 10pt Plantin by Bryan Williamson, Frome
Printed and bound in England by SRP Ltd, Exeter

For Diana

Acknowledgements

Some of these poems have appeared in *Brangle, Honest Ulsterman, PN Review, Poetry Wales, Thumbscrew, JAAM (New Zealand), Jellyfish Cupful, Magdalen Poets*. 'Corncrake' was originally issued as a Sycamore Press postcard illustrated by Julian Bell. Those friends, and two in particular, who have kept me to this task with their encouragement know who they are and know my gratitude. But I have especially to thank more recently Brian Hinton for astute and heartening comments on an ur-draft; Tim Kendall of *Thumbscrew*; and Jonathan Williams for inspirational support for this and its related project *An Aran Keening*.

Contents

Plato's Aviary

'Miss Kershaw would identify the bird as the bar-tailed godwit or "yarwhelp" . . . the godwit being called "yarwhelp" because it resembles the curlew.'

Ida Gordon, footnote to *The Seafarer*

(i) NEVERMORE

The ravens we knew cast no shadow then,
Honking and cronking over the bryn
Head-over-heels in courtship's light
-hearted flight at first of spring.

Wheeling so high, they went out into orbit
Somewhere beyond the cwm,
A shadow falling only after
All these years, like light from stars.

(ii) GREY-LAGS (*Anser anser*)

for Sheila Pehrson (née *McNeillie*)

They so rarely reach here now
You'd be forgiven for thinking you're dreaming,
The dream of eternity, or some such,
You with your goose-wing westward prospect,
And a puddle blowing at your door:

Demisting your spectacles in a cloud of linen,
Squinting across the flapping morning
To see how their true aim's flown,
With an arrow-head as variable as any head,
Wavering in a smudged heaven.

(iii) WHEATEAR (*Oenanthe oenanthe*)

As if those walkers could be troubled
Distracted from their confidences
To leave the path and cast in circles
After your decoying loops and glances
From stone to stone among
The bleached and thinning grasses
To find your clutch
Cupped at the heart of silence here.

As if even one of them could name you
Or know you by your stony chatter
But you rehearse regardless
To be on the safe side
Of this shadowed mountain till
Kingdom come as once below
Time was the people sang
Their hearts out everlasting.

11

(iv) CORNCRAKE (*or* LANDRAIL *Crex crex*)

Spring slips him in through a gap
In a stone wall, a secret agent

Bargaining with the underworld
Against sleep, a bomb

With a slow time-fuse, an old man
Winding all our clocks on, and back.

(v) CURLEW (*Numenius arquata*)

So burdened with sorrow that
Its beak is bowed down by it:
A Campbell mouth, *whaup* in my lost lexicon.
But of leaden skies on the moor
The virtuoso elegist, even in spring:
Always the one I want to hear again.

Last night I dreamt I woke
With one beside me, its head upon the pillow,
Eye serenely closed, and, however dark its dream,
I saw at once that it was really smiling,
Not grieving, but upside down,
So as not to give the game away.

(vi) TERNS (Common and Arctic, *Sterna hirundo* and *macrura*)

Rule of three? Escapees from Matisse,
Playing scissors-paper-stone along the beach.
Who'd second-guess you but by luck?
Not this raised strand of storm-stressed shingle
Petered to sand where your pebble eggs lie nestled.
Not summer's page of vanishing blue
So slow to unfold its origami of stars.
And not these thole-pinned oars that snip a wake of puddle
Litter where you mob and scold, and dive
For fry, and I spin my line to the bay.
Maybe only the quicksilver dune that's never still,
Shimmering grain on grain, can match
Your lightning wing-blades? So odd
You seem to have chosen me to halo,
Who haven't an earthly, with my two wooden oars,
Not even now you're flown, wherever it is
You fly to, and I have all the time in the world.

(vii) LAPWING (*or* PEEWIT *Vanellus vanellus*)

You cannot will them back, but why,
when I can recall at will
their lapping sorcery,
to the precise peet or peewit
of their billowed flight,
should this empty morning's grey
bowl of sky above the farmland
remind me first of the one
that landed in our hearth
on Christmas day, uncrestfallen,
soot green-black and white
with metal legs and feet
and wings you might
operate by pulling on a wire?
a decoy from the continent, a gift,
an ornament, a childish toy to us,
that had us charmed,
if never for a moment fooled –
when I'd much sooner think of them
in their magician's night-and-day-
under-over-plover-cover-lapping light,
and sing them, as we then could,
tumbling over the winter wheat,
making the air throb, their wings
in mittens for the cold, their crazy wits
rivals to the mad March hare,
as now to me, in sorrow,
shadow boxing here.

(viii) ADERYN DU (Blackbird *Turdus merula*)
i.m. Hughie Bach

No more a soul of fixed abode:
Missing, though seen upon the road –
The low road high in blowing weather,
The low road to the racing river –
Ardent for nothing but his loss.

Bare branches and wild sky god bless:
Tenebrous blackbird on the gusting air,
Where October's river, hole-in-corner,
Digs deep to drown the depths of winter,
And sings its own intoxicating song.

His warning spills out hurriedly, as if
He has withdrawal jitters from the demon drink.
Alarmed again, he scolds away
To skulk through shadow on shadow
Along the memory of spring.

(ix) ANOTHER TAKE ON THE BLACKBIRD

In the rocky rowan the blackbird sings
Tunes from his golden treasury
His pall-grave book of poems,
Turning phrases this way and that
In the thin leaves and evening air,
Miraculously, his eye transfixed.
His song an obolus for the ferryman.

(x) GODWIT (*Limosa limosa* or *lapponica*)

Waders splinter light, in sudden galaxies,
And surf echoes hooves, along the metalled road,
Fainter and louder, starlight in each breaker,
And the heavy dune dashes its grasses,
Its crests of marram, breaking into
A wall of light, in a heaven harbouring
Wonder at the anchored moment,
On a morning charged with spring.

Where everything seems surging to become,
I tug from the jetsam this earthbound one,
Salt-dried stiff and weightless but
Unmistakable, god knows: a godwit,
Witless, but whether a black- or a bar-tailed,
It's already flown too far away to tell.

(xi) WREN (*Troglodytes troglodytes*)

What poetry? Wired up out of light and dark,
At the mercy of seasons, genie or Houdini,
No respecter of persons: a wing and a prayer,
Seat of your pants kind of affair? Uncrowned king
Of obscurity, your music as pungent as ivy?
No fear at those great shades whose project is
To float off cathedrals and symphonies
Over the abyss and limbo there for eternity,
Consoling, constellation beyond constellation of loss,
In your little local speech of stars
And saplings and crepuscular melancholy,
A line of solder silver between sky and holly?
A tin-pot holding operation, a quick fix?
My little winter communard, sleeping how many to a bed?

(xii) CORMORANT (*Phalacrocorax carbo*)
for Ian McNeillie

I remember the day the old man shot one
high over the house and how it folded,
like a winded umbrella, and came down
in a thorn bush, stone dead, neck collapsed,
wings hooked up to dry for the last time.
But why still, the nervous, apprehensive wonder,
the word *skart* on my tongue for pleasure?
Why couldn't I settle to sleep that night
for thinking about it? I wasn't upset.
I didn't weep. It got what was coming to it.
It was the devil, the thief on the cross, of fish
that we might catch. Way out of range it swerved,
but the old man was a dead-eyed dick.
I'd seen him perform such miracles before.
And even if I smiled, when he laid it out
for my education in the life and death
of birds, and distinguished it from the *SHAG*,
I kept my school-yard smirk to myself, so he had
no cause to curse me for a tom fool.
Perhaps it was just those three dabs,
the size of half-a-crown, that came
flipping from its gullet alive, alive O
O, O as moist as eyes? . . . Maybe.

(xiii) LITTLE STINT (*Calidris minuta*)

Stint your step to spring, unstinting,
Quick to cloud and lose yourselves
In shell-bursts, treble-voiced,
Suddenly reunited, for a stint ashore
At the storm's edge and limpid
Aftermath of the streaming strand,
The fine grains timing you
At your ankles, piping cold,
Time's stinted passage in the harsh tide.
So I come here to shiver with you
And chatter in the dying day
Of loss untold, taken at the flood.

(xiv) CHOUGH (*Coracia pyrrhocorax*)

Considering their distribution in old haunts
Of armadas where even the people
Can still bear an Iberian look, I'd like to believe
These crazy *kiaow-k'chuf* kazooers embody souls
Of red-lipped girls descended from flamenco dancers,
Or Catalonian cross-dressers in black skirts and
Red stockings, fled from the Inquisition,
Castanets clacking, castaway to flirt on cliffs
And strut their stuff above the wrecked Atlantic.

Though the authorities say the truth is other and
A while after all roads led to Caesar's Rome,
Or Ovid's exile, the soul of King Arthur
Migrated into one, which would as well explain
Why choughs are so fay and flighty, being
Deranged and déraciné just like me, with
My binocular visions, captive to a dream
I have lost and gained in being here before them
This day beside myself with pleasure?

(xv) WOODCOCK (*Scolopax rusticola*)

Blued gunmetal dusk conducts cold lightning
To my memory. In my blue hand then
The barrel of an Xmas pen, in a snap below freezing,
Brings you to that coast and me to myself again,
At eighteen, bedroomed to the creaking wood.
Shall I dream there for you, with guilt in my heart,
Cleaved as lightning to gunmetal? Like lightning
Your anticipated flight from the dead leaves,
Leafmeal and leavings, traceries of snow:
Little maps to get blear-eyed in, staring and
Staring crepuscule, stalking moccasin to look into
Your big black eyes too luminous my love to
Hide you, the flaw in your camouflage and
Sober bearing. Shall I fail to find you or in a
Snapshot catch you as you jink out through
The empty saplings into star-dust, blown
To the ends of the earth? Or turn instead and
Meet you *roding* by, growling like a toad,
Then tutting *tsiwick tsiwick*, at just an arm's length
In purring flight between the yew and hazel,
Your long bill pointing as if pensive at the ground:
So that even with only half my wits about me
I might reach out and catch you in my hand?

Here is the field of grass in shadow
With its bare hedge and gloomy oak.
None receives the sky but stands off
In winter mirk that will soon turn
Dark. The world's shut down like
A risky Chernobyl in whose full glare
We might all die but for this precaution,
Though die we do of seasonal boredom.

Here I recall my youth's captivity:
Just in this spot and at this hour
Out to escape the inescapable,
Mooching in fields and woods,
Half-watching a shadow-world fail
When at the corner of his Northern eye
Wings the herald, fast, with snow
And storm in stars upon its breast.

Life will change, but whether
For better or worse, take heart,
Such sudden flights and bitter-
sweet termini beneath mistle-
toe or holly wreath, are bonuses
Forever, second-looked, named twice,
Once seen never to be forgotten:
Mistle-thrush or Stormcock.

(xvii) JACKDAW (*Corvus monedula*)
   for John and Sheila McNeillie

O local shades, so much more like us than
The others, in your community and accent,
Loyalties and squabbles: good neighbours,
Chapel folk, field-workers, quarriers
And gossips, cackling all day *ky-ky* mozaic
Music to our domestic ears, routines
And little ceremonies of hearth and ash
And fallen soot, swelling to sudden
Blissful crescendi and shimmer above
The wooded bryn, now heard and
Forever through the heart's high roof.

Believe me, since we co-tenanted Coed Coch
Or that seaborne life at Tan-yr-allt,
I've travelled ways and worlds as far
As birdless Acheron and back, would strike
Your poor hearts dumb, for thirty years as I
Have been, sea-green corruptible, in love
With setting out, the better to know home
The moment I first hear you greet the day.

(xviii) YELLOWHAMMER (*Emberiza citrinella*)

The first telephone we had in our house
presided in Cyclopean silence, at the foot of the stairs.
Its big dial stared at us as we passed
as if daring us to make a call. But to whom?
It had about as much use as the front room.
But unlike that soot-scented holy of holies
it was for us ahead of its time.
For some reason its mouthpiece made me
think of the dentist, or the colossal
lower mandible of a fruit-eating tropic bird
seen in the waiting-room's *National Geographic.*
Listen deeply? I can still hear its silence,
waiting, and its shopdoor tinkle
as I lift the receiver from its cradle,
its seductive purring tone.

But ours was more like a clunky country girl,
with its plaited brown cable, on an
outpost farm, waiting for a call.
Until it came, I used to dream it might
resound with spring's hedgerow and wall-top drone
where the stave of wires hummed its backing
to a limpid lyric: the yellow-hammer's
deil, deil, deil, deil, tak ye, curse squiggled too
on its egg in the roadside nest I knew
where the holly grew in with the hazel;
or that *a little bit of bread and no
cheese* (the cheese sometimes omitted as
the authorities say; as if to show evolution in
process). But then there came other birds.
Deil, deil, deil, deil, tak ye.

26

(xix) TEAL (*Anas crecca*)

The proper term for this activity is roding.
Beneath the flat stare of the moon,
In from the scything estuary to glean
Or flock around fresh water,
Thick, and quick as any jump-jet wader.

Here shoots up a solitary, in exclamation.
Not saying where it came from, just
Announcing already that it's almost gone?
To disprove that one can
Ever stand for many, many a one?

As some would like to claim acclaiming
Self, and they'd be wrong,
The truth of teal and true poems being
For roder as for reader
That they know no comparison.

(xx) REDWING (*Turdus musicus*)

This Sunday walking in the park I saw you,
Frozen still, as if you meant to melt from view
Before my eyes, resisting my subpoena,
As one might cut a former lover's gaze.
But witness you must stand now none the less
To purely circumstantial evidence of loss, such as:
A youth's Cold War affair with Julie Christie,
Upon a soft and saline coast in nineteen-sixty-
something, when snow as never seen since
I don't know when fell, fast and thick,
Across the heart's Siberia, a blizzard of pages torn
From a scene by Pasternak? And plodding home
The long way, for the hell of it, he met
An epic flight of heralds, overtaken by their own foreboding.
Their calls so close to *SEE! SEE! SEE! SEE!*
Made him look up to where they milled among
The flakes and fluttered in the little wood,
To perch exhausted, or fall down dazed, their eyes
Within eyes already blank, at the farthest gates.
Reds with the stare of Strelnikov, harried by the elements.
Too late, however you regard it now, to speak
Of innocence or snow. The two he succoured
With codliver drops and airing-cupboard billets
Died in their socks, should you care to know,
Redwing in the park, this February morning.

(xxi) BULLFINCH (*Pyrrhula pyrrhula*)

A true poem about you would
Make no mention of apple or bud.
It would be far too fly for that.

Just the premonition of them and
You would vanish with a blush
That somehow managed to be brazen

Leaving the ripped promise of fruit
And us perversely at the window still
Longing for you to be so bold again.

(xxii) WATER-RAIL (*Rallus acquaticus*)

As well try to walk on water
As hope to see you with my
Stalking eye and stealthy
Halted step in imitation of
Your freeze-frame motion.
But somehow in your beady
Look, the mirror-echo
Wetland of my heart
Catches a miraculous sighting.

Complicity of hunter and
Quarry they say: the one
Willing to become the other.
Up front at last and audible
Where water changes into sky
Sky clouds and turns to ink,
Foot by foot, I hold on to
Your broken railing and
Advance into the reeds.

(xxiii) GROUSE (*Lagopus scoticus*)

How did you get that lipstick on your eyebrow? So
Lavishly she kissed me in those days.

Grouse? I've no more grievance than Arenig
Head-in-cloud, dreaming of a dawning moor.

In that feral time I came of age and world now
Gone, over the hill and under it, flying in the dark

The peat-dark of this inglorious flesh
And bog-soft dram, served me on my birthday.

Day Star

The outhouse lamp left on across the yard.
A farewell taken only last evening for a greeting.
Light years away it seems now, ushered out
In night-holm's evergreen aftermath.

So much hope, so little time?
Galaxies in the wings. May I share them with you?
As the Bear said to the Plough, the trick being
To suspend belief in mere appearances of things.

Sluggit: An Augury

Now in that fallen suburb
They birdwatch so avidly
Last year a neighbour swore
He'd heard a songthrush sing.
And so such things are now heard,
Darkling, without witnesses.

As too its sister immortal:
The jugging nightingale
That sang in Greek;
The Latin-speaking landrail;
All such fugitive lives
And voices in our archipelago.

Juno and the Peacocks

A peacock's fan of stars shakes
In the empty trees; and winter rocks
Its cradle loud enough to wake
The coast, but folk tuck down
Like roosting birds and cuddle up
Close together: let slates slither
And windows rattle. This is the time
For headstrong dreams, or was,
As now only dreamt and longed for:
Consider this bird fable of
Lives enriched by dreams alone.

The three of us set out that night,
We lookout brothers and the old man
On a moonless, lunatic adventure:
To steal Lord Mostyn's peacock
From its sleep of galaxies and
Poems, as a rare gift for my mother.
The peafowl slept in yew-tree shadow
Upon the Estate wall, but facing out,
Their tell-tale tails within the pale:
Considering the fable of their lives
Enriched by dreams alone?

What peacock vanity! as he reached up
To pin its shoulders and to take
Its legs, and hurry homewards.
Just so, its startled neighbour woke
To cry the peacock's jungle cry
And rattle up to the rattling wood
Its train splayed by the storm.
While now at home the peacock men
Were brought to earth by a plain peahen:
To consider the fable of their lives
Enriched by dreams alone.

Passeriformes

These of course are the true ones.
Every time they pitch into their songs
Of love and space it's perfect music.

If they falter it's because someone came in late
Or coughed or shadowed the sun,
Or a rival upstart redstart trespassed.

Listen forever to them all
But beware the enslavement of memory
In their instant cadences.

Wedding Snaps with Hoopoe

A bridesmaid in her cinnamon pink
Cranes to watch the bouquet fly,
A shuttlecock of luck she's pleased to miss?
As birdshit hits the terrace table. Hoots of laughter.
Another day for her, to sip the tart champagne of love.

Confetti blows, as if already the stuffing leaked out of them,
Through holes the size of buttonholes,
Shot in the back; the shutters spray, as they make
For the ribboned limousine,
Blossom dancing on wings in their wake.

A last glance back through the beady lens at us,
And what it awaits, let no one put asunder.
The coital bliss. The heart's tristesse.
The I do. The voodoo. The hoopoe under the verandah.
Its variegated plumage and erectile crest.

Elegy

Why so many birds in the bare branches of your poems
flitting like titmice on a spring morning high in the pines?
Along your rivers and shores or plummeting down windswept skies,
tagged with Latin like shrubs, trailing banners like planes,
advertising the end of the world, or speaking Welsh? A parliament
of fowls in an age hardly rated for its inclination to govern, sing or
    rhyme
however inflected, or confected, of however many blackbirds,
or even warble, let alone boom, or caw, or coo, or honk, or hoot,
    or quack,
whoop, mimic, mewl, wail, shriek, pee-wit, or, crexing, ratchet back
the winding stars all night beneath your window,
a breath in the curtain and the moon a sea-green halo,
and the depth-charged surf full of wheeling, phosphorescent notes
    of waders.

In the hope you might imagine a world without them:
no thrush on the aerial; no yellowhammer on the droning wire,
begging for a little bit of bread and no cheese, on the back-roads now
only of memory; no wren's loud voice in the winter ivy;
no chaffinch on the coldest morning ever recorded for March;
no wild swan whooping from the windswept lochan;
no ousel deafened by the stream's spring force;
no lark ascending, no redbreast whistling, no parrot either,
in Amazon or parlour. Not one. Not anywhere, ever,
heard or seen, of this or any other feather. Mourn them?
They mourn themselves, their ghosts soaring from the lost glades,
the crashing canopies, rocketing on startled wings.

37

Reservoir Boys

The whole village siphoned its spirit,
brewed it and bathed in its quick-to-lather
softness, said to be bad for the heart,
but so good for theirs, pulsing water,
spilling light, who knew its shores,
cupped on thin air, in the cwm's high cauldron.
Rest the heel of your hand on its cold tap,
numb to feel how, under ice, it welled
down in the deep close season, when,
fish nosing the damp spense, or press,
of his heart, he dreamt a smell of oilskin
and dried-out net sequined with scales,
a torn mesh caught with gauze,
wardrobe of some drowned dream's ballroom:
shades of the Winter Gardens and Saturday's big sisters
out to rock their handbags steady,
till midnight rolled over, calling:
where have those girls got to?
And other mysteries held in reserve
awaiting spring's remote rainbow
to frame their innocence at last.

The Whiting
for Graham McNeillie

Snow falls when you least expect it.
A rural saying to amuse the sceptic.
But none the less
A clichéd Christmas greeting
Fooled the coast that year
With stinging flakes, as perished flocks
Of redwing refugees in comas
Fell dying through the silent branches,
Out of Scandinavia,
Or a northern elsewhere, anyway,
Its serrated horizon of pines
Sawing the blue cold of a brief day,
As glimpsed at the Odeon
By Sharif's Zhivago.

That day we went to the pier-head
And fished all evening in a yellow storm.
As if to show
How dreams-come-true
Establish norms, the whiting rose
In blizzards from below
And stormed our hooks
At every single throw
Until they skidded round our boots
In translucent lobes of ice
Their eyes like melting snow.

Extras

Never a Joseph, nor even a shepherd or wise man
but some surly angel, train-bearer,
or escort to a king, without a line to spin,
to fill a tableau or swell a curtain call,
so fitting them for life far better than
brief village stardom might. *Enter, shuffling,*
as if nudged into view by war's statistics:
History's full-backs and reserves.
Cannon fodder talent-spotted early.

Learning Difficulties

Light rises from the page
like an evaporation, from laboured letters:
as when showers pass and sun emerges
the pitch roof steams.
The school echoes sporadic voices,
shouts, whistles, PE in the yard.
His eye balks at phonemes?
It has to do with cues and codes?
Holding his pencil in his left hand?
Half the girls are on book six
oozing success and speed like sex.
They think he's as thick as his chapped legs,
still fast in the midden
with *Old Lob* a lout consigned
upto his burning ears all year,
hearing the others adventure
with chicken-licken, goose-loose
and all that rhyming crowd
hurrying off to tell the king.
What's wrong? He doesn't know.
They tug his blubbing heart away
to dens he keeps at Pentre Uchaf.
To oaks and acorns, chicks and eggs.
His sky has fallen and he glowers
with wounds and fears.
No comfort to him he can count
the long hours, the long years
that lie between him and his name.

Raiders of the Lost Heinkel

Nothing their youthful granite hearts
Could grieve for when
Evening filled the air with stillness
And turning from the shore they
Cricked their necks to see the wreck.

Gott in himmel!
Those fifties Nazis swore
High overhead, limping, lost:
Achtung, achtung!
In misty billows droning

With finger-tips describing
Arcs across the spurting shingle
Ack-ack, ack-ack . . .
Their comic cuts
Streaming from their lips like clouds . . .

No language for the tragic night,
As, never for an instant foreseeing,
Altometer fazed by valley and lake,
Or on the blink, they smashed,
A dazzled moth buckled on a screen

Smack into the crag forever,
A Roman candle exploding stars
And as soon burnt out,
The years ahead, piled up behind;
A botched Goering memorial

By *Airfix*: fin, aileron, fusilage,
Swastikas and camouflage,
In minutest detail: tears
Before bedtime, gluey globules,
Gathering a wardrobe's dust.

What might have flashed through their minds?
A joke? Some sepia lover's name in mufti,
Multiform, and tender? Time without end,
Searching for words like mother or father
Or just the German for 'Oh Fuck!'?

As those boys swore, and searched, and found
Among the bilberries and heather
Nuggets and leaves of aluminium,
A treasured light-bulb, weightless
As midges treading air, their souls dancing.

As Sure As Eggs Is Eggs

The old man's collection in two flat shortbread tins,
their 'shellacked' cardboard sections graded from
hoodie to wren, from pre-war Scotland, gave me
a head's start over the others, in that brief season
of pious inspections, and judicious theft: never more
than a single egg from any clutch, blown dry
and relocated, in individual nests of cotton wool.
None of it more outrageous than that afternoon
an indignant butcher's son sat on a cuckoo chick
to avenge the dunnock. What were we like?
Vigilantes, eugenicists, murderers, hypocrites?
Or aesthetes? Connoisseurs of nest construction,
the function of materials, lichen, moss, mud . . .
dilettantes of eggs as heavenly as the stars, in all
their patternings and colours: materialists merely
Platonists by other means, our days in leaf-shadow?
So in freckled youth, I mooched about my business,
prying on the progress of the greenfinch in the holly,
climbing torn into the hawthorn, on a sullen afternoon,
to play magpie to the magpie, or tailing a wagtail
Upstream. Then, when I got home, last light still in
the trees and hedges, no verdict on me but to say:
boys will be boys, their hearts as wild as spring?

Lampreys

They writhed at my feet, snake-like,
eel-like, as if hooked, and so they were,
leopard tails switching in their lust to breed,
in a dance you might call the *lampreda* or
lampetra, in the Latin vein, 'the stone-sucker',
each with its jawless mouth and rasping teeth
limpet-fast. Thirteen I saw there clearing stones
the size of bricks, pebbles, gravel,
to make their redds and lay their eggs
for the males to sperm. Then one turned to me
where I stood unpartnered and we danced.
Suckered to my wellington, she drew me deeper
down into their weaving spell, that dappled
day, the river low, and no salmon running.
And I went, my best foot forward, mesmerised,
as if they added me to my sudden knowledge of them,
in a mysterious ritual, like those dance-night girls
I knew by name but could only crave
as they shuffled to and fro, boogying together,
until one beckoned with a look for me to ask her.

In Memory of Private Roberts:
British Soldier
for Eirwen, Ann and Wyn

Crossing the square in early spring,
Wreaths withered on the memorial,
Poppies bled by frost and snow,
I met Private Roberts reading
The roll call of the town's fallen.

'Armistice day? My pet aversion,'
Turning to me, his lip moist,
His thorny eye narrowed like a sniper's:
'Ior Evans? He'd never spent
A night away from home before,

Buried in Mad-a-gas-car.
Corner of a foreign field?
I doubt he'd ever heard of it.
Dei Sam? on Manchester
United's books in thirty-nine:

Buried in France. I bet
He's never remembered
At the going down of the sun
Or in the morning . . . Duw!
You know, I often contemplate

Siegfried Sassoon, chucking his medal away.
Never applied for mine.
All the way to Tobruk without
So much as a lance-jack's stripe,
I'm proud to say.

And Francis Ledwidge, born
The same day as Hedd Wyn,
And killed, you know, the same day
And in the same place too.
His comment: "To be called

A British soldier
While my country has
No place among nations. . .'"
He'd marched to Vesuvius
With Marcus Aurelius

In one breast-pocket and
The *Mabinogi* in the other,
An old campaigner
Over bog and heather
To find and fish the Serw stream:

Elusive, stubborn thread of water,
Of stygian glooms and mountain glances,
Its limpid, garrulous medium,
'Full,' as he said, 'of small trout
The length of a youth's hand.'

A Childish Bear

If there came a point when
They stopped being divided at
Road forks but knew as if
By gravity the way for them
Was determined by the shortest line
Between two stars, or as many
Angles as it takes to plough
A field or draw a childish bear,
Or to stride to war, or to steer from
Fishing ground to harbour in a storm,
From drinking hole to farm:
If there came such a point
You can be sure they never could
Put a finger on it any more than
You can though you know
The name of every point and star
In the neighbourhood
And every bird and every song.

So, when you come home
(Too rarely to convince?)
From home and meet them
Before that horizon of headland
And sea, awaiting night's crown
Of thorny stars to chasten the heart
To its core – as if you were
The curlew crying *quee quee quee quee*,
The traitor on the battle moor *corwee* –
And the bare forked hawthorn,
Its hair combed out on gusting air
Above a bank of henna'd bracken
Raising its arms to heavens
Where arrow-heads of geese
Target your already unbearable losses
(The girl who broke your heart)
And the spick white holding
Holds on to the hill
Tenaciously, as if for you,
A bequest you decline to accept,
(Losing to possess), word-play

48

The name of the game for you:
Once, twice, and thrice upon a time –
What seems like deference
Is just their patience waiting
To snap shut on the slightest
Indication of presumption?

For sure, they're keeping watch
To tell again with every day
The dark side of their idyll
The moment you betray the
Moment, you betray the love
They hold here now for you
A lease beyond tomorrow
When once again (for another year?)
They stand waving you out
Of sight and into mind where
Meanings seed and reseed
Thistles and cockles and grief
At never being even one remove
But always at least two from
Anything you'd call belonging
Anything you'd call the truth.

Ancestors

'In this great future you can't forget your past'

BOB MARLEY

In cases they're cameo memories,
In others relics. Ghosts that stalk
With looks for voices so we'll say
Things like, 'Oh she's the spit of her mother',
Of someone far away.

Photos and letters, a tree of names,
The old man keeps for me:
A peasant tribe whose sober praise
That so-and-so feared god and spoke plain
Shadowed their daily mockery.

We savour one's defiance of
The local aristocracy.
Recall that same man's ignorance
Who, in our era still,
Saw in a son's prospective bride:

'A good breeding woman' –
As if a heifer or a mare . . .
Redundant necessities
And orphan luxuries, they are
Poles unlike for likings to attract

Our longings and losses,
Our narrow northern dooms,
Like it or not. Like it and not
To kick over their traces
With all our meanings

Must be our lives
That others will not know
And better know better
Our sins and crimes
Still waiting to be named.

Dreaming the Iceberg

So conditional upon unknowns true dreams
are rewards only patience may claim part in
be it at midnight or mid-morning, whenever,
where what I mean by true is otherness that
tells a tale as sound as any worked up in
the light of waking and what I mean by dream
is light itself beyond all the days and nights of
the world as touching on each angle for example

in the iceberg that I hooked last night while
delivered of a dream as clear as crystal
casting surf for bass below a winter's lintel
of ice-cold points with starry ears and nose
and frozen hands until what then appeared to vex
my heart was a dilemma whether to cut loose
and save my line for later as literally an angler would
or land it if I could and risk that it might melt my gaze.

Hair of the Dog

Rain, one-hundred per cent proof,
Intoxicates the windblown day
But doesn't keep us from our thirst,
Or make us face another way.
We plod on through the shite,
Collars up and tails down,
Addicts too of gravity and light.

On the longest binge since Noah's ark
It swells the river torrent here
Searching out old pockets for
Tumbling leaves of gold and silver,
To stand around at the road's elbow
In a froth-lipped gesture at largesse,
Digging deep, the drunken bore.

Plus ça change . . . it loves to seep.
But here's enough small change
To get us dry, for a hair of the dog
To bite with light the flinty drop,
To pause with you a moist lip,
A moist eye, and raise a glass:
To the dog. To the drowned dog.

Realities

You do not need to be dumb
To be rendered speechless.
You do not need your theft hand severed
To find writing impossible.
You do not need an objective correlative
To spend Christmas in a murderous mood.
You do not need the literal
To compose the real.
What is it then my friend I need?
I give you in one:
Your heart's desire.

Late Bird

In October's thinning light
He's twittering a Platonic sol-fa
Paler than his notes in spring.

He's lost it, or found it?
Sapped to the dark root-tree
Under winter's early stars.

Meditation in a Public Garden

'Ce chien est à moi, disoient ces pauvres enfants;
c'est là ma place au soleil: voilà commencement et
l'image de l'usurpation de toute la terre.'

PASCAL, *Pensées*

Rendezvous for respite here? No way.
Melancholy the shade of gravel and the fountain
Wavering its *fleur-de-lys'* imperfect heart.
This world waits for me as if I was myself
Procured, a rare but dim shrub with a Latin
Name, dogsomething dubbed by Linnaeus, say,
And planted on a damp bench between
Leguminosae and *Cistacea*; in their case both
Damned to mourn a Mediterranean soil and sky
For life as I mourn love and youth
Unnoticed in my grief by either as they pass,
Arm-in-arm, or pause in front of me to kiss.
What flesh! To be elsewhere if I could for once
Not a guest like this at my own urn-burial,
Cheek the colour of white bread and paste,
Funeral meats, a feast of endless asphodel ahead?
There's life-pulse in the veined leaf yet,
Protest, if not enough to prompt a second look,
To make one stoop and take that tender
Sapiens sapiens label for a wonder (planted in '46!). O,
If we were creatures in a zoo, we would express
Our sadness in pacing round and round. But I
Just sit here staring at my hands, salve not slave,
Or who could bear not to look into my eyes?
Salve to my every grief and conscience?
My heart, this scant bush rocking to and fro,
Winds back upon itself like the wild rose.
But get up and go, you fool, follow your nose,
And have a gander while you can, from
Alp to Tropic, rock to hothouse rim,
And admit pleasure in this imperium?:
Over seas and under other stars than these,
For the time of year, stars that already
Prick the sky with subterranean light
From somewhere long ago, to the South,
Where pithy men I would not like, with all

Their equipage in train, lend everything
They can a name, if possible, their own,
From stick to stone, from sprig to State,
Until there is no other world to legislate.
The reason I come here, to be alone,
Unclassified, and without my maker,
To pursue a poem with pen and paper:
Against the grain, in homage to Anon.

Post-Colonial Study

Here in a clearing strange tribespeople
Dust off their charms and fetishes
Shakespeare & Co, *et cetera et cetera*
And all those names from here to Derrida,
Sit elbow-to-elbow round a table,
Ejected from a forest idyll:
The brilliance of its exfoliating shades
The wild notes of its paradisal birds
Its super-subtle scented airs
Its snakes and spiders, lions and tigers,
Taxonomies, laws, courts, and favours –
An extinct mythology, a library
Besieged within a failing citadel
Searching for new premises.
Language swarming at its honeyed hive
Failing to get through the eye of the needle.

Silence Please & Be Upstanding

The day is silenced by the night,
The palace garden by a banquet,
The agents by their cover.
The dark is silenced by the moon,
The minister's mistress by her lover.
The room is silenced by a spoon
Tinkling a glass balloon.
Silence, please, and be upstanding.
Silence is an oxymoron.
Whose ghost is that upon the landing?
The state is silenced by its fear
Like princes silenced in a tower.
Cain silences Abel. Babel babel.
Light silences the star.
The spider spins in silence for the fly.
The tortoise silences the hare,
Timon Athens, Caesar Rome.
It's in the silence that it happens.
The Black Man, silenced by the White Man,
Hangs in silence from the tree.
Silence sanctions tyranny.
The sky is silenced by the sea.
A storm silences the promontory.
Silence in the wilderness is loud,
Elsewhere it stuns a crowd.
Nuremberg is silenced by a hand.
The words are silenced by the mind.
Serbia silences and . . . vice versa, Serbia.
The woods are silenced by the guns.
The soldiery are silenced by their wounds.
The birds are silenced by their songs.
(All's quiet on the western front.)
The lie is silenced by the lay.
Who'd silence poets may
Grant them immortality.
A poem is silenced by a commentary?
(I think not. Therefore I am.)
The church is silenced by a prayer.
Silence is the thing you vow.
Supplicants are silenced by the host,

Murderers by a Hamlet's or a Banquo's ghost.
We pass into the greater Silence.
The quick are silenced by the dead.
The dead are silenced by the quick.
The rest my friend is history, or not.
Silence fears how Denmarks rot.
Her love is silenced by pyjamas.
The ape is silenced by bananas.
Silence wall to wall surrounds us.
The truth is silenced by the family.
The lovers' toils are silenced by
Half-past-one in the morning.
It is a very silent feeling.
Staring in silence at the ceiling.
As silent at least as breathing.
So silence keeps the night awake
And in our dreams we hear it speak
How night is silenced by the day.

Wish List

The iceberg that makes it round the world.
The complete works of Anon.
A cape and stars above the sea.
The camel through a needle's eye.
The Life of William Shakespeare by Himself.
The first of day. Her louch look.
The sweetest fuck.
The nesting bird.
The omertà of old age.
The light at the heart of the pyramid.
The song you have by heart.
The harbour light at dawn.
The sound within the poem.
The curlew on the moor.
The wild-goose skein.
The raven rolling in a windy sky.
The world turned upside down.
Tête à tête avec Owain Glyndŵr.
Genius-in-waiting.
Winter lightning.
The last word of the old order and first of the new.
The Republic of Scotland.
The Republic of Wales.
Vision and revision.
Hindsight as foresight.
The reader read.
The people's voice.
The happy couple.
The oar's puddle.
The Tower of Babel.
The lighthouse bell.
A millpond sea.
The dune's crest in the moving air.
The tribe's oral tradition.
The other as me.
The one in B minor. The next line.
The coelacanth's mating ritual.

The girl who never returned your love.
The end of all that. The end of all this.
A new poetics. A new prosody.
The poet guilty as charged.

Lines from An Aran Journal
for Gail & James McNeillie

A docu-poem in homage to J.M. Synge and
Tristan Corbière to be read aloud

'I am in Ireland now; now I am at a third
Remove.'

Gerard Manley Hopkins

I heard him through the floorboards and
sea-view windows of my tidal youth:
kept one eye on the poet, the other up the chimney
looking at the stars, in a madness like first love,
for dreams and words, the material word.
Swimming before my eyes, the curraghs plied their sticks,
c-u-double oar-a-g-h, stable and
unstable of meaning, in that small volume,
from Maunsel, Dublin (only half the story to hand),
tipped my balance and under I went,
drowning, drowning, overboard.
Deathwish in the offing. Maybe?

Now I'm remembering it to you;
in this belated verbal voyage
riding the word-flood of my own sea-pastoral adventure,
in the wake of a notebook litter of pages
blowing eternally behind the *Naomh Eanna,*★
the ghost without the machine.
As if on waters never sailed before (as I read now in Dante).
Will you know me in time, by my stitching,
by the ribbed pattern of my story washed ashore?

It is for you I sail again, upon these pages,
by broken compass, at October's ending,
from moonlit Mersey, to Liffey dawning,
sharp and shadowed, blue and starry;
aged twenty-two, with all my worldly goods,
and thee bestow (heart's stow-away) the fool,
by storm-blown train to Corrib's flood

★ *Naomh Eanna* pronounced *Nave Aynia*

and Galway, grey city of the thirteenth tribe.
Its raw boys cry *Try-bune, Try-bune* still
down Shop Street and Eyre Square,
'For Faith and Fatherland' with news I note
of wedding bells and fatstock prices,
a Connemara pony (Ballroom Door-prize)
at Saturday Night's Talk of the Town;
and tinker girls and mothers beg
'A couple of coppers' outside Naughton's:
in the teeth of a rattling gale, blasted
non-stop from Nantucket and Cape Cod.
There to kill time at the Atlantic Hotel,
asleep to the Shipping Forecast, at 0:100 hrs,
Shannon, Rockall, and Malin Head . . . Storm 10,
dreaming of the islands, and their denizens,
spare lives among tall waves and stories.

There's Tom Feaney foetal, man of extremes,
where extremities go hand in hand:
matter and mind at the edge of the world,
his sister Maggie and the Yank, his brother,
sunk in sleep, within life's sleep;
and other, immemorial Toms and Margarets;
Grannys and Sonnys (of recent memory);
Marys, Patricks, Martins, Aines,
Brians, Daras, Stephens, and Michaels;
and that legendary tribe the Twenties, all
deep in their mysteries, silent as Sicilians,
O'Kosans and MacCalors,
in the omertà of the small hours:
rocked to sleep on a roller coaster
dreams muffled by the stormy blather –
a mare run loose upon the road
galloping from Killeaney to Bungowla,
while out on the rocks a hundred yards of drystone's flattened
                                    at eighty-miles-an-hour.
Their fishing fleet rides out the night
lost in a leeward haven, or loops the loop,
keels-to-heaven like the stricken *Ard Aengus*
off Mutton Island, whirled to disaster,
running aground near Glassin Rocks:
Thomas Conneely of Kilronan,

John Michael Gill, and John Faherty,
owing their lives to the *Star of Faith*
and Mr Pat Jennings of Long Walk, Galway,
to say nothing of their maker.

And what if long-shanked Tom
in his upturned craft should wake
for a leak? He can count saints as others
count sheep, six score at least, to recover oblivion,
flyting the blacksmith on the road.
'St Enna, St Benedict and St Giban,'
the smith hammers; Tom riding by calls back:
'St Fursey, St Conall and St Brendan of Birr.'
'St Berchen . . . St Kiernan . . . and MacLongius . . .'
the smith's riposte meeting Tom's parry:
'St Cathrodhochus . . . Assurnaidhe, . . . and Brecin . . .'
as they fall from earshot, and Tom snores –
among more saints than are dreamt of in
your average philosophy, Aeneas on your battlements,
where the heavens and the serpent sea, winding
and unwinding, concentrate the mind on
four last things: sanctity and virtue,
guinness (for *veritas*) and, double-edged, dole

on a Tuesday.

Day of his landfall, out of the storm,
from Rosaveal airborne, aboard the Ard Colm*:*
up the airy mountain, down the rushy glen,
gale-force 9 gusting storm-force 10.

The fool in his dream-days, postponing
the world, like one of Dante's hawkers,
peeping through wild sea foliage,
no Virgil or Statius to call him away,
to more becoming business:
hostis to fortune, the stranger, dazed,
among tea-chests and cylinders of gas,
guinness-alloy drinking up the dregs of light –
staring about him, on Kilronan quay,
a waterlogged seabird blinking an eye –
as if just surfaced from the crack at Kenny's

or Conneely's American, dole-full,
and drunk as November's Atlantic sky.

Now evening's failing and night's on the wing:
a night of Tam O'Shanters, east and west,
on rattling bicycles or ringing hooves,
clattering the roads and boreens
heads full of wind-scattered stars,
the lost diaspora of dole day,
missing presumed drowned in the black of night,
aswim with guinness as they haul at last
into their plunging beds, between Finistère and Bloody Foreland:

To snore themselves awake into the past
of a pristine morning and aftermath aubade, at peep of day,
in a notation to rhapsodize forty shades
of grey, fractured to exquisite colour,
anatomies of stone and light, stone fields of light,
or pampered sea-loam-sand-loam, hoarded for harvest,
the brimming shock of bleached rye gone but
potatoes still for clamping, in tombs of rusted bracken;
as the hours tick round the cambered sky,
measured by tide and light, lunar phases
in a moonscape of pavings and glacial leavings,
marched by walls and honeycombed,
smoking rain and spume and wild geese in clouds,
a winter hothouse, in a sea of shattered panes,
blooming primroses and gentians, come Christmas Eve.

There the village rides into the morning
in its ruin: half-deserted, half-renewed,
its pattern of property and labour skewed –
fugitive, a mere trace, part-memory,
part-necessity, mapped to the unravelling strand,
where rights to harvest seaweed hold in a few heads, or submerge
        and drown.
Here, a native returned with his family,
bringing young laughter like faulty memory;
an exile back from Boston, dying of cancer;
a crone and her brothers; a modern landlady,
her guests long flown with autumn's migrants;
a workaholic bachelor, his faith in land;

a Pioneer maid, her faith in the Lord;
a labourer's love-child, skipping on a doorstep:
shame and ostracism, in a settlement
of a dozen homes and a nest of ruins.
(Curse the sinning priest to hell and back,
may he dig his grave in the field of the horse.)

'Man of Aran? Don't give me that.
Mickey Mouse and Donald Duck,
that's your Man of Aran now.
The Last of the Mohicans had
a better future than the likes of us,
boots or no boots . . .' So Michael mocks.

They're on the strand and on the rocks
without much scope to lead two lives, unless
they hit the rocky road to build another,
nightwatch in Chicago or Manhattan,
to learn the heart's ambiguous hunger.
They're on the quay or on the sea while I'm
in his white-mane pages, his trammel nets
of words and hooked lines, spilleting the Sound,
of thirty years his strangeness never landed –
beyond clocktime now, keeping tidal hours,
coals leavened with driftwood's peacock tails
of vivid mineral, mantle purring,
he's looking to breakfast off fresh ling
before Craghalmon's gulls pirate his lines.

And writes, while he waits, the Crusoe-circuit of his day,
as I write for you, pirating his lines,
into the small hours, on a high; his motto
'To authenticate' and find the thought in things
he sees and things the people do – cable,
diamond, trellis, moss, honeycomb, fern,
zigzag, trinity, and tree-of-life: riddles for you, unwritten
and unique, to knit the soul together,
against the hour, against the weather.
And the storm-tide's harvest of kelp, ribbon and claw:
wave-deep, man-deep, disgorged about their boots:
sea-weed for the cultivation of roots,
panniered by dromedary across the rushing strand.

Sea-candles dried will fetch £13 a ton
in the manufacture of 'Ladies' stockings, out in Holland'
(and Scottish toothpaste, to polish up your grin,
or lipstick to lead you back to sin),
gathered for half a year, and more,
wind-dried-to-all-but-weightless mauve-black bundles,
haunted by summer's sandflies: patient labour of Pat Whiteley
who learnt the hard way how
'There's nothing for nothing'.

The watches of the night are long and growing longer.
When is the dawn? When will the thinning day begin?
The seas are high and growing higher.
Stir-crazy bachelors are waxing crazier.
The mails are late, the trawler somewhere stranded.
Supplies are scarce. The steamer's out of service
and they're charging 'double-freight'.
There is no news of any real moment.
God to you. God and Mary to you.
Tom's headed east in Sunday best, for a funeral in Killeaney.
God to you. God and Mary to you.
Kate Whiteley's lost six pullets and suspects
the stranger. But he's oblivious of any fowl
or any foul play, and notes in his journal how
he dined on tinned crab and soda-bread today.

How little does he know what his doom holds.

* * *

INTERLUDE
He's dreamt too well in feverish delirium?
He's drunk too much on Christmas Eve?
He found a message in a bottle?
He caught the clap off a girl in the Claddagh?
Nurses are writing patients' stories down.
They've got him there, in Galway Hospital.
'Did you eat at all?' 'Did you pass water?'
asks the doctor now. 'D'you mean a bridge?'
puzzles one grizzled codger, eyes staring.
But the playboy, your fool, 's fallen fast asleep,
lying heavier than the sands of the sea,

67

temperature up and abdomen tender,
he dreams he's sailing the *Naomh Eanna*
200,000 miles high, around the moon,
in the wake of the eighth Apollo Spacecraft.

He'll slip back down into orbit at last
to the elysian strain of accordion music,
a snare-drum rapped and rolled, a fiddle and a whistle,
playing jigs and reels; doctors and nurses,
priests and visitors, and walking wounded,
surge up and down the aisle, one of them
calling for Sir Roger de Coverley!
Sir Roger de Coverley! who's nowhere to be found.

He thinks that he's died and gone to heaven.
Two tinker boys stand by his bed and chant:
The wran, the wran, the king of all birds
St Stephen's day got caught in the furze
So up with the kettle and down with the pan
And give us a penny to bury the wran.
And proffer him a small waxed box for harps to play
and hounds and hares to chase in the wake of the wren.

His *largesse* earns him another stirring stanza:
Dreolin, dreolin where's your nest,
It's in the tree that I love best.
In the tree, the holly tree,
Where all the boys do follow me.
So up with the kettle and down with the pan
And give us a penny to bury the wran.

Then one from Inishmaan comes in to know
is he the man from Aran? (He is so.)
'I'm out of it these three weeks since,' he said.
He fell after a wake and tapped his head.
'They did find me in the morning. Nothing I knew at all
but the next thing was, I was in this place.'
Loughrea's Pat Burke raving, fights to go home
to milk the cows at two in the morning
and curses his sons' passion for dancing.
Everywhere memory, in and out of vision,
wanting still the art of recollection.

I am his loss but do my level best
in steep rainstorm, and sharp hailstone,
to discharge as he sails home, on January 4, 1969,
my duty to him and his long poem.

★ ★ ★

No prodigal's reception for him but
a commotion of curses and goads,
flailing arms and skidding hooves –
to repel him and his scribbling eye,
its trespasses and appropriations?
There's Tom sold the fatted calf, palm still moist,
to a Galway jobber. It swings up high
in a sling from quay to hold, bellowing
to a bleak sky, on that leaden morning
of farewell, and tears, as schools start.
The girls gather astern, waving,
and, as they cross the bar of Aran, shriek
in a single orchestrated keening,
so shrill and clear it stops the day
to dwell upon exile, past and future,
or hope lost, and boats missed.

But January is the women's month
for conspicuous pleasure and consumption.
Their hearts delight to hit the waves
for grey Galway's rock-bottom sales.

And though winter's yet to come, in February,
with biting frost from dawn to dusk,
and storm and fog and sinking gloom of submarine shadow
(crustacean consciousness, unmentionable sexuality)
hearts lift up to unwrap new crockery:
bed-linen, carpets, oil-cloth, cutlery . . .
that was a time the *Naomh Eanna* retreated,
two hours out, off the storm-swept Burren;
two hours in and the women all but rioted
waking to find themselves where they'd started.
O how they railled! O how they doubted
the captain's manhood, scolding like fishwives,
stranded with their shopping on Galway pier.

But hearts lift up to light and will not be put back.
The last goose cloud hangs high on frosty air.
He's more at home, and less, as days draw out
inchmeal to seedtime. But still the sea
bucks, and kicks, in winter coat and will not
take a rider readily, or nurse his nightlines.
They're on the shore and in the fields, digging.
One man they say turns over twice what two men do a day.
Above the blowing Atlantic, talk's free and time
by the mile runs, as far as eye can see.
Many missed boats, and many losses.

'Somebody has to stay,' says Michael.
'That's how it is here now, that kind of way,'
turning his back to dig.

And before they know it the lazy beds
are sprouting haulms. Or there's blight on
the damp June air, calling for 'burgundy mixture',
calling up the starving shades of hunger.
They're at the fair, they're at the races.
They're playing jarvey on the pilgrim's road.
They're singing songs, they're telling stories.
'Three days and nights with a dead man in a curragh.
Before the waves washed us up
on the coast of County Clare . . .'
At Conneely's American, tourists are teased:
'You must contribute or you cannot leave . . .'
And as the door is barred a tipsy schoolmaster
stands up to sing an English hymn,
his nervous Adam's apple keeping time.
They're dancing jigs. They're squaring up to fight:
Marcuses and Daras, Stephens and Anthonys –
Dig your grave! May you suffocate and drown! –
while the grey cuckoo calls to the mackerel sea.
And the corncrake's winding on the clocks
and winding back the hours and stars and stars.
The corncrake, rare to see, as sleep is hard to find
when he is on the prowl beneath your window, going . . .

crex crex crex crex crex crex crex crex crex crex
crex crex crex crex crex crex crex crex crex
crex crex crex crex crex crex crex crex
crex crex crex crex crex crex crex
crex crex crex crex crex crex
crex crex crex crex crex
crex crex crex crex
crex crex crex
crex crex
crex
crex crex
crex crex crex
crex crex crex crex
crex crex crex crex crex
crex crex crex crex crex crex
crex crex crex crex crex crex crex
crex crex crex crex crex crex crex crex
crex crex crex crex crex crex crex crex crex
crex crex crex crex crex crex crex crex crex crex. . .

Hour after hour, to and fro.
And where is he? Elusive bird himself,
crexing round his pages, rare to see?
O don't ask me . . . He's out all hours.

He's two legs of six in a pantomime beetle:
rock-hopping a curragh with Tom and Michael
to the moon-risen tide, at Bungowla,
pulling their sticks through the Callagh,
America to port, on seas stacked to heaven,
another rite of passage for him:
out to lobster, after the wedding,
hangovers swirling, daylight sinking,
their black barque skimming beneath new stars,
short waves off the Brannogues.

He's out with Tom to break the Grey Fella
to harness, cart, and metalled road.
Their heads cartwheel home all full of talk,
and grating rims and skidding hooves,
scribbled in the ink of guinness,
the night like a day, as Tom said, and the island

71

a thorn-patched moon of tangled shadow.
And as the year's wheeled round, from holy day
to holy day, he's everyday out on the rocks, to fish,
casting and recasting, working to land
Dara's Englished oral Irish dirge and
nineteenth-century priestly homily,

YOUNG-GRASSES ROCK

I
One autumn morning
When all was sweet
No malice in the wind or air,
The glorious sun
Shone warm and genial,
Gently disposed
To the whole wide world.

II
It was the feast of Glorious Mary,
The year of 1852,
When a crowd of young men
Bold and quick,
Went fishing at
Young-grasses Rock.

III
They saw a great mound
Moving near them,
Easy and lazy,
A clumsy sea-monster:
A powerful wave
That now bore boldly down.

IV
Nor did they think as need was
To make it from the shore
But tended to their tackle
Till the rocks ran with a roar,
And met the power
Of the leaping wave.

V

Alas! was no escaping
The vile wild wave that hung
Heavy on high above the rocks,
And all the brave men doomed
Upon the flagstones drowned.

VI

Its power now bent and broken
Upon the flagstones bare,
The wave sank home:
My thousand sorrows' care
But it went not empty.

VII

For it swept upon the fierce edge
Fifteen men in the flower of bravery,
Leaving sorrow and tears
And heartbreak to
The people of Killeaney.

VIII

Sorrow and torment
In Killeaney that day,
As fathers, mothers
And loving relations,
Mournful and demented,
Wept and lamented,
Keening the strong men
Who'd never return.

IX

Early they rose that morning
Cheerful and strong,
Filled with hope
And light of heart,
But to lay happiness
Upon a bier
Before night fell.

X
O here is a sign to heed,
To judge not what is before us
Or put our souls in pawn,
For we must save the harvest
Before our hour be flown.

XI
Who knows in what place
Or on what shore
Death will come
To sweep him on his way?
So we must be upon our guard
And ready for the day.

XII
That tragedy our lesson
Swift and sudden
Upon Young-grasses Rock,
Their souls swept to heaven
Lost in the sleep of life.

(Mac an Fidlih *fecit*)

★ ★ ★

Ready for the day? As sure as death.
The *Naomh Eanna* to sweep him on his way
and plough the waves with his blowing pages,
his sea-green truth outstaring my pedestrian *trahison* –
my ghost, his Synge-song, my swan-song
homage, read through thirty years unstable,
the nature of time and space we could not meet.

More

(i) ODYSSEUS AT KILMURVEY

The road taken a sea-road, harboured at heart,
Sea-green corruptible as Plato would have said.
How even now there's uplift in the thought and
Sinking, and slide and backslide, unstable dancing
In the tide's gift and weather's frown or grace.

Time alone will tell. In a snatched week's solitude,
These driftwood planks and spewed spars thrown
Down here make a start. Time alone.
To go the longest way round, via Holyhead,
Is to take the shortest way home, the man said?

My poor temperament is slight and prone
To gabble *ar lan y môr* like geese on a stubble,
A sea-stubble of threshed waves I imagine
Off Wales now. Too big for words,
The sea hasn't aged since earth began

No more its guiding lights of inert stars,
Flickering from the sunny universe above.
All resolution to be resolute mends and breaks
Like the sea and holds like it. My heart
In an embrace now of stars as sharp as whins.

Starlike too, gulls wheel and cry with light on fire
Above the crackling coast and harry heaven.
And as I go, or think of going, a sadness weighs anchor,
To find Tom Hernon dead or in his island garden?
Never go back they say, never return.

As if you could – when and to what?
Except to the drowning sea itself off Connacht-know-nothing.
I stand as he did and not as he did.
Chasten me and my sojourn baptise
Leaden sky, this side the dark strand.

75

Youth knows what it cannot tell and now
My telling is forgetting. To remember: I am
Already and always somewhere else, and
So are they. Time's worn us beyond recognition
Since those days? You would not believe.

Keep your threadbare name to yourself
And play the strategist for once.
Just a word told here will be a truth at least,
Sound as a pebble in the shingle. Did you ever know
A friend I had lived here? (I never did.)

Thirty years is a lifetime in your wake and many lives
And many fares to many fairs. No voyage without a wake
And no death worthy of the name: when did you last see daybreak?
Who plies your journey now? Who tells your stories? *Naomh Eanna*
    I pray for you
And all who sailed in you on those wild seas I knew.
Though just whatever comes to hand may decree what's beautiful

In time: transports of delight now make Magic of the Sea
(*Draoicht na Farraige*): *Flyer, Sprinter, Express* . . .
By Australia out of Disney, or that light plane from
Connemara Regional Airport with its Special Offer of
A 'Return from Anywhere' should that be where you
Choose to start from, longest way round shortest home.

I saw it start that summer of '69 prospecting for a runway
And now it makes a short way home in planes of light
Exquisite as any then that cast their spell across the evening
That fateful summer of unrest on Derry streets, written
On walls no one then could read from far-off Inis Mór
Itself hand in hand with poverty and hand to mouth:

Most of all exports in her lading, summer's big-boned youth.
Even you there, with your suitcase, in your best blue suit,
Wanted by the Gardai for GBH, slipping aboard like Theoklýmenos,
Who killed a cousin once on an island not entirely unlike this in
    Ancient Greece.
Where are you now, I wonder, where did your days wash up
Since I aided and abetted your escape that heart-rent morning?

I never saw it start and will not see it end but to my dying day
Naomh Eanna in your name more than any other let me pray
Sailing down the breakers' yard on the highest winter tide
For those in peril: all who may fail to find their love at last
Returned at such an hour as this the island ushers in
Where all the elements make landfall, here and now, at once

lým

The day long. Though pleasure's nothing without the long shadow
To which it is the silver lining briefly unfurled and furled
Like an ensign, a national flag even, in a gaunt dawnlight,
As when I saw them in the Sound, the Irish Navy sinister and fleet
Come out of nowhere, the Corvette *Cliona* firing a round
To intercept the Brittany trawler *Gars de la Pointe*

Unlawfully fishing in Irish territorial waters (fined £20.00
In Galway Court). I am the Ireland they're fighting for,
They might claim could they have claimed to speak for Inis Mór.
But who'd make so bold in any court, by guinness or by god,
Among you, unconversant cousins of the Sicilian O'Mertàs,
O'Kosans and MacCalors, locked in your sad vendettas? Still?

What will I find among you now? Memories as sharp as my own
In which I figure merely as the dimmest recollection, even to myself,
Lost soul pilgrim playboy in the wilderness in love with seascapes
And fish-hooks? Escapes and wish-lists? O dear Tom and Margaret,
Should I find you living, all that, and time, will fold into the moment
As when eyes or palms meet in greeting or in parting or in prayer.

O steady witness, *Naomh Eanna*, mute ferry of how many dooms,
Tides and weathers, fair days and foul, with your high prow
And low saloon: when that last time lands for making good escape,
May I come over the island's shoulder and find you and the others
        waiting,
Straining at the pierhead, and cattle loading to propitiate the gods,
And a course set never to make landfall anywhere but here again.

(iii) CUCKOO (*Cuculus canorus*)
Bungowla, Inishmore, 22 May 2000

Those binocular vowels O O
With which from drystone walls
You spy the land and play
The two stops of your double life
Otherwise so singular:

Pipping pipits to the post,
Dunning dunnocks for a down-payment,
What is it with you
On your short wings, like
A hawk at dusk?

O O only turn coins over at
Your bidding and nothing
Want from May to May,
Is comfort I suppose to those
Who like to play away?

Who've written you out of any
Truth and into their feeble guilt,
As if those zeros were lenses
In opera glasses trained
On Don Giovanni.

But tonight around this
Drystone filigree on air
As delicate as any sung,
All turned to light, I hear
The pair of you in stereo

Begun: whirring and purring,
In frenzied ecstasy.
Something else, as they say, worth
Keeping to yourself: O sing,
Cuckoo, and louder, sing.

(iv) A TUNE FOR BLIND SOUND

Some new-wave band into synaesthesia?
In those days nothing of the kind
Would have entered my mind
Tuned as I was to wave-bands more like
Windrows in Sonny's meadow then,
Down where fastidious mullet
Fished the weed and flotsam
And mackerel stormed at the point,
All summer as the tide turned and
Crept round the clock of my fate.

But what if I'd known then what
I know now? Would I have smiled?
Would I have wept? Would I have
Waved on ahead, and cried: Wait for me!
I may not know what I'm doing
But you'll find it has meaning for you
By the time you catch up with me,
For by then that's the way it'll go:
With the tide turned and
The clock fast that was slow.

(v) A LETTER HOME: IN MEMORY OF THE CORNCRAKE
Kilronan, 23/4 May 2000

I've just blown in and the word seeps out
like rain puzzling the window with
a jigsaw view, bumpy and blurred.
I quartered off whole acres of stone
and sea this afternoon and then met
Tom himself, come riding down
on a mountain bike, behind his collie.
He's seventy-six, still keeps a pony
and some cattle, his eye just a little
rheumy, but his back still straight. I
puzzled him all right, balding and
burlier than the playboy ever looked to become.

After so long there's everything
and nothing to be said. The roll-call
of the dead, who married whom,
how many kids they had. He keeps
the same regime but hasn't taken drink
these past six years. Poor Margaret
had a stroke but is now improving.
Her memory not good. Next morning
with a sickle he went cutting briars,
foursquare methodical, as I remember him,
in his peaked cap, making a cock of each clump.
He didn't look up as I passed; his
buff gardening gloves, a telling sign
how much those times are past.
But nothing's missing to my mind
or his. He lives to a philosophy,
on what he knows is borrowed time,
working as he always did, but when
he leaves these days, he takes the plane,
as when he dies he'll go to heaven.

I worry what we're going to do for talk.
There are gaps here in the evening.
There always were, you know, but not
gaps into which I did the talking.
Gaps in walls. Gaps, though now

the dead outgrow the plot, and that's
with two men lost at sea:
Mikey McDonough, Brian O'Flaherty,
aboard *The Lively Lady*.
They searched the Sound for days.
I said there's nothing missing but
nothing concentrates the mind so
absolutely as to speak too soon.
Some pieces strangely seem to travel.
Facts meet where they didn't before.
And grief has its day once more.

It wouldn't stop raining that night
and the cuckoos wouldn't stop calling,
until gone ten and eleven o'clock.
I've never heard the like. But no more
than ever I could, could I keep indoors,
rain or no rain, boots or no boots (not
quite): I walked out like a gentleman, in
gortex coat and over-trousers,
poking the road with a stick,
a rare vagrant passing through,
going up and down, and round about,
from dune to cliff, from bay to Sound,
in the dark: a jig-saw on a loopy circuit,
as the fine rain fell and rinsed the rocks
and filled the air with pungent scent
of seaweed. I thought it was only
a matter of time, and so it was
underneath, before I'd hear one
marching to that old crex crex.
But all I heard was a silence that grew
the more I heard it, until it drowned
everything, drowned all the world,
silenced the whole Atlantic shore, like
a stopped clock, and no one I met
could remember when, how long ago,
the spring failed, as if one evening,
of old age. They were expected but
they didn't come and life is different.

Marcus driving in his trap to meet the boat
all down a dazzled morning, salt-breeze
and sun, high drift of cloud, stops for me
and takes me to Kilronan, by the low road,
for the longer *craic*, of this and that:
Marcus the Roman, Roman name and nose,
but Hector and Achilles in one, those days,
bare-knuckle pugilist, King of the West,
now in round sixty-three, up against age,
who'll take him the distance.
Wild, wild Marcus, who loved his guinness
but it's no more black stuff, either, now.
Doctor's orders, until the world goes dark.
Graduate from fisherman to jarvey
(classic progress), with stints between,
in Birmingham and the Isle of Grain,
he'll take Yanks for a ride all summer,
telling them the old old story. He's
humoured how the commonplace fascinates
them: 'There's a water tank,' he points,
a corporate umbrella handy, in the event
of rain, 'There's another water tank . . . We do say,
but sure, we're not interested in them.
We see enough of them, like,' he grins.
Seals play in the ebb below Mainistir and
sea-birds in the air, everywhere perform
at the borders of the picture, where
the blue pieces of sea and sky seem
interchangeable, as life for death,
in a dream departure to unknowing.

As on my final morning. The harbour
in a bustle, and Mourteen having
searched each day to catch me, stops
in his red van on the causeway.
O causeway to what ending? I
can see the youth in the man yet,
father with a family, skipper now,
rival to the Spaniard, in and out of Killibegs.
What's the fuss? (The mini-bus jarveys
are on their mobiles.) Everyone's in it
for once, as all the fishing boats make ready

to sail in convoy out to escort in
the *Shauna Ann*, deep-sea addition to the fleet,
first new boat since . . . ? none could
remember when. Not surely, I thought,
since the *Ard Aengus* (grounded and
wrecked near Glassin Rocks in '68)?
Out they sail beyond Straw Island
and bring her home, under an
arch of flares, in the grey easterly morning.
The women shrill like gulls, the jarvies
sound their horns, as she comes to berth,
some old enactment surviving, flipside of grief.
But there now the *Draoicht na Farraige*,
and no more my love the *Naomh Eanna*,
strains to be gone. And so once more,
in the quick linking of wave into wave,
to the last piece of horizon, I begin to scrawl again
WITH LOVE, THE END

(vi) CLEARANCE
i.m. Annie Hernon

It is too late for some things,
No use arguing with that.
I should clear my head here now
As one day they cleared out
Stuff beneath the roof in that
Old store: spinning wheel,
Loom (engines of the fates),
Dresser, and drift nets.

But the wind off the Atlantic's
Not enough it seems, nor all
Its glare, like new whitewash,
Narrowing eyes, as when
She smiled. Now she's closed
To everything, like an answer,
Who always shrewdly kept you
Guessing what she thought.

(vii) PORRIDGE

Putters softly in the pot like a horse
Trotting down the island in the dawn.

Pan grates at the hob, shoe to road, as we wait.
And round the bleary eye a sleep of oat-film dries.

Rims of the barrow grind, their spokes mill,
Round and round, as we turn.

Light shines bright as grain in the cold air.
Ring of hooves now and husks of late stars.

The sea ripens, shoal upon shoal for harvest,
And we're off to a good start, memory lined again.

(viii) TO THE *NAOMH EANNA*
      FOUND RUSTING IN CHARLOTTE QUAY
      26 May 2000

Lost among the Dublin quays I found you lost and might not
had I not been lost, by chance, and late about to miss my sailing.
I was your lover once but turned and lost you in the crowd
of stormy seas, and skies too strong for gulls, that day you stood me up
in wild November. They said you'd gone to Dublin then
for a Board of Trade survey. I accepted there were other
men in your life, in every port, and hit the drunken skies by trawler.
But this time, lost in my thirty-year-long labyrinth, and quays,
and old warehousing, and far from thinking of you, I turned and,
suddenly: I saw you, up against the wall. The eye is forever young.
I knew you. For proof I had a camera. But my camera had no film in.
I had to fly or miss my sailing. This was a fleeting fate who else
could share in, now, among the living, and fathom to its end,
and call to mind such sailing we had known, of waves and seabirds
at coming home or leaving: circumlunar, making headway as
making love, on any B or C sailing: home via the islands or
via the islands returning? I knew you, at first sight, unnamed,
through all decay, my sight so young. But we've no hope of ever sailing
now, unless aboard a poem like this, at the harbour wall,
already rusting, and both of us too late for it: not sailing, just listing,
in a basin. Dank reflection, just off Pearse Street, and all Dublin
sailing past us as we fail, the breeze in your rigging frail
compared with those Atlantic gales, when the islands
heaved at their mooring, and your high prow so proud,
pitched prouder than ever, in the brunt of the weather,
that I cannot quite believe my eyes I ever saw you, then or now.

Notes

PLATO'S AVIARY
In Plato's *Theaetetus* Socrates uses the aviary as a figure for the mind, the nature of knowledge, and the processes of knowing and of recall, or, as these unsystematic poems loosely interpret it, memory and recollection.

'*Curlew*'
My father once told me that the mouth of a Campbell starts under his nose and ends at his arse. In gaelic the name means 'crooked mouth'. 'Whaup' is a Scots word for curlew – as in Whauphill, a knowe where curlews used to gather in the autumn, not far from North Clutag farm, in Wigtownshire in the ancient kingdom of Galloway. Born and brought up in Wales, as I was, as a boy and youth I romanticised my Scottish heritage very desperately, and fetishised words like 'whaup' and 'cleg' (horsefly) and 'scart' (see below) as they fell occasionally from my father's lips, like crumbs from the bread of truth.

'*Cormorant*'
To the McNeillie family, tenants at North Clutag, the cormorant, crossing as it might between the shore and the Bladnoch river, was known as a 'Mochrum scart', a cormorant from the coastal village of Mochrum, sometime home also of McNeillies. 'Scart', which in my youthful mind was spelt with a 'k', is a derogatory term meaning a base creature that scratches, and scrapes after food, as you might greedily scrape at a dish with a spoon. Though the cormorant in this poem was Welsh.

IN MEMORY OF PRIVATE ROBERTS: BRITISH SOLDIER
An elegy to E. Meirion Roberts, native of Penllyn (Bala), prominent Welsh Nationalist, artist, illustrator, autodidact, fisherman, and Bard, sometime of Hen Golwyn, my birthplace. The memorial referred to stands in the square at Penllyn, and the dead named in the poem, all former residents of Arenig Terrace, are identifiable among the fallen listed there. Penllyn and Llyn Tegid (Bala Lake) are key locations in the Mabinogi.

LINES FROM AN ARAN JOURNAL
This drunk and disorderly documentary poem derives from a prose memoir, *An Aran Keening: Adventures in the Western World* (Lilliput Press Ltd, Dublin). Some sixty-thousand words long and finally written up as a cautionary tale for my children, it is itself drawn from a journal, and from letters I wrote during a sojourn on Inishmore, Co. Galway, November 1968 –September 1969.

MORE
These eight poems were written in anticipation of, during, and finally after, a return visit in May 2000 to Inishmore. They celebrate again the world portrayed in 'Lines from an Aran Journal', but more than thirty years later.